UNBELIEVABLE!

34 AMAZING FACTS ABOUT SPACE

Marie-Therese Miller

Lerner Publications ◆ Minneapolis

To my daughter Erin, the family rocket scientist, who is working on the Artemis program

Lerner Publications Company
An imprint of Lerner Publishing Group, Inc.
241 First Avenue North
Minneapolis, MN 55401 USA

For reading levels and more information, look up this title at www.lernerbooks.com.

Main body text set in ITC Franklin Gothic Std.
Typeface provided by Adobe Systems.

Editor: Annie Zheng **Designer:** Mary Ross

Library of Congress Cataloging-in-Publication Data

Names: Miller, Marie-Therese, author.
Title: 34 amazing facts about space / Marie-Therese Miller.
Other titles: Thirty-four amazing facts about space
Description: Minneapolis, MN : Lerner Publications, [2024] | Series: UpDog books. Unbelievable! | Includes bibliographical references and index. | Audience: Ages 8–11 | Audience: Grades 2–3 | Summary: "Space holds some of the universe's biggest mysteries. Readers will discover incredible facts about moon missions, planets, stars, and more in this fun, high-interest book"— Provided by publisher.
Identifiers: LCCN 2023013880 (print) | LCCN 2023013881 (ebook) | ISBN 9798765609040 (library binding) | ISBN 9798765625170 (paperback) | ISBN 9798765619025 (epub)
Subjects: LCSH: Astronomy—Juvenile literature. | Solar system—Juvenile literature. | Outer space—Exploration—Juvenile literature. | BISAC: JUVENILE NONFICTION / Science & Nature / Astronomy
Classification: LCC QB46 .M556 2024 (print) | LCC QB46 (ebook) | DDC 520—dc23/eng20230722

LC record available at https://lccn.loc.gov/2023013880
LC ebook record available at https://lccn.loc.gov/2023013881

Manufactured in the United States of America
1-1009536-51582-6/15/2023

Table of Contents

EXPLORING SPACE

The Apollo 11 crew flew to the moon in 1969.

Edwin "Buzz" Aldrin

Its crew members Neil Armstrong and Edwin "Buzz" Aldrin became the first people to walk on the moon on July 20, 1969.

NASA's rover Perseverance landed on Mars on February 18, 2021.

The rover collects rock and soil samples.

The Artemis program plans to send the first woman and first person of color to orbit the moon in 2024.

Artemis will also build a moon base camp.

Up Next!

PLANETS IN OUR SOLAR SYSTEM.

PLANETS

Jupiter's Great Red Spot is a spinning storm that is hundreds of years old.

Great Red Spot

It is wider than Earth.

Venus rotates in the opposite direction of Earth.

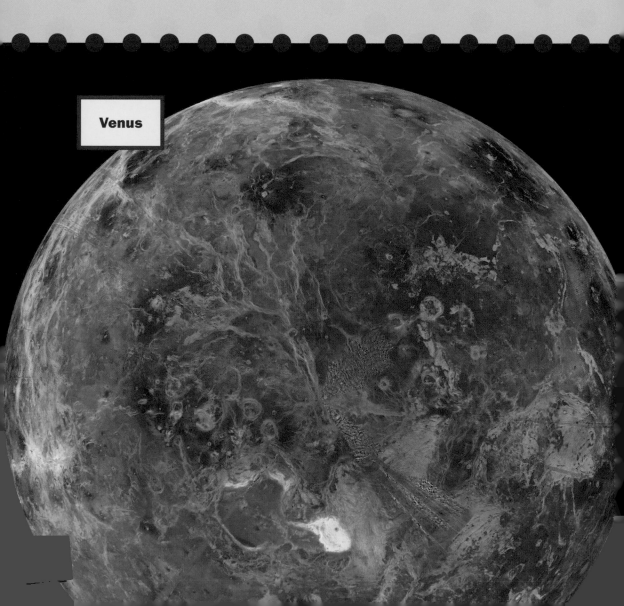

Venus

Venus

Venus spins slowly. One Venus day equals 243 Earth days.

Uranus rotates at almost a ninety-degree angle. It appears to spin on its side.

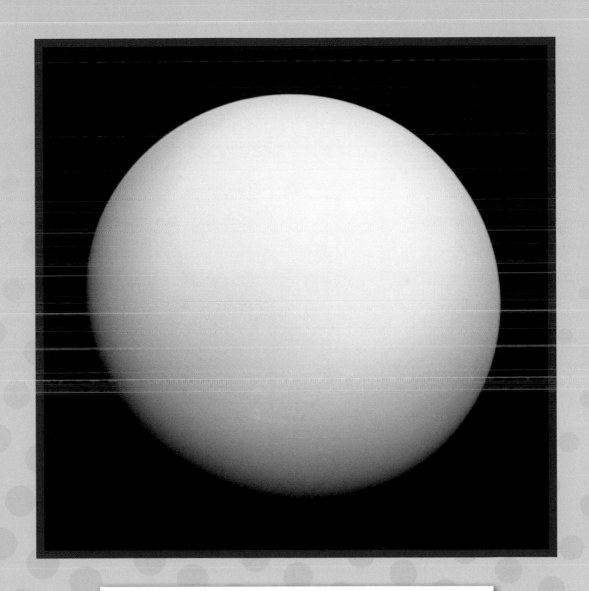

Methane, a gas in Uranus's atmosphere, gives the planet a blue-green color.

LIST BREAK!

Here are the five hottest planets in our solar system:

1.	Venus	867°F (464°C)
2.	Mercury	333°F (167°C)
3.	Earth	59°F (15°C)
4.	Mars	−85°F (−65°C)
5.	Jupiter	−166°F (−110°C)

Mercury

Here are the five planets in our solar system with the most moons:

1. Saturn   146
2. Jupiter   95
3. Uranus   27
4. Neptune   14
5. Mars   2

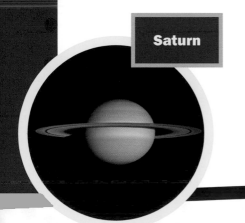

Saturn

Up Next!

A LOOK AT THE MOON.

EARTH'S MOON

The moon reflects the sun's light.

A lunar eclipse occurs when Earth is between a full moon and the sun, and Earth's shadow falls on the moon.

Comet

Meteorites, asteroids, and comets leave craters on the moon.

The craters are nearly permanent because there is no wind or rain to erode them.

Scientists have found water ice on the moon.

The ice is located at its north and south poles.

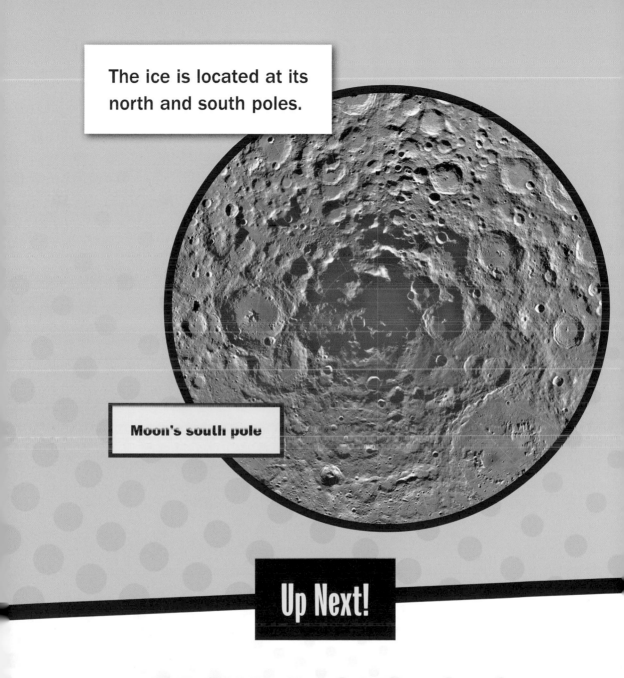

Moon's south pole

Up Next!

THE SUN, SUPERNOVAS, AND BLACK HOLES.

THE SUN AND MORE

Earth's sun is a yellow dwarf star.

Its core temperature is 27 million°F (15 million°C)!

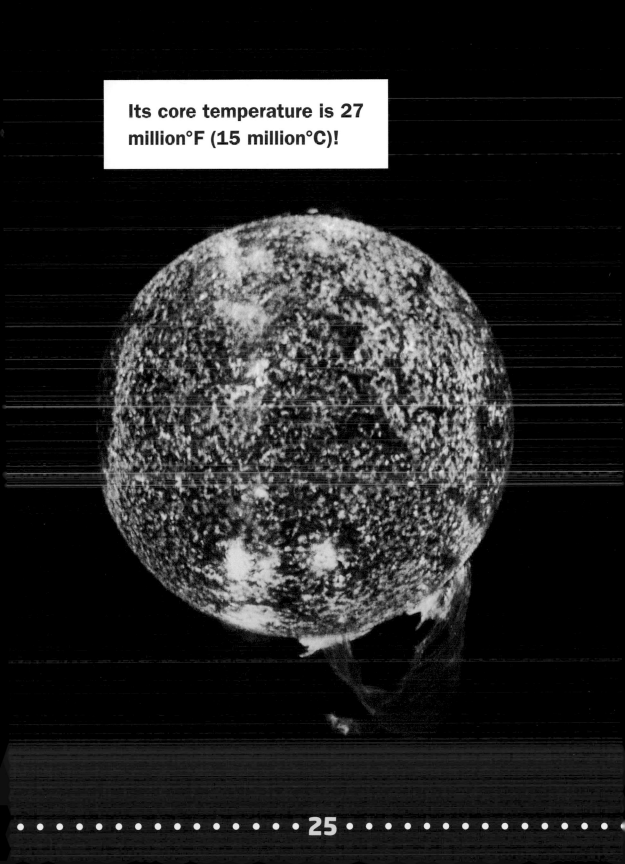

When most big stars
die, they explode.

Supernova

This event is called a supernova.

Black holes have gravity so strong that even light can't escape.

Objects are stretched long and thin near a black hole. This is called spaghettification.

Glossary

atmosphere: the layer of gases that surrounds a planet

crater: a hole in the ground formed by an impact, such as from a meteorite

erode: to wear away gradually

rotate: to spin

yellow dwarf star: a medium-sized star

Check It Out!

American Museum of Natural History: Astronomy
https://www.amnh.org/explore/ology/astronomy

Golusky, Jackie. *Weird Space*. Minneapolis: Lerner Publications, 2024.

Morrison, Marie. *20 Things You Didn't Know about Astronomy*. New York: PowerKids, 2023.

Murray, Julie. *History of NASA*. Minneapolis: Abdo Zoom, 2022.

NASA Space Place
https://spaceplace.nasa.gov

National Geographic Kids: Passport to Space
https://kids.nationalgeographic.com/space

Index

Photo Acknowledgments

Image credits: NASA, pp. 4, 5, 8, 10, 16, 27; NASA/JPL-Caltech, pp. 6. 7, 11, 12, 15; ESA/P. Carril, p. 9; NASA/JPL-Caltech/Wikimedia Commons, p. 13; joshimerbin/Shutterstock, p. 14; NASA/JPL/Space Science Institute, p. 17 (Saturn); NASA/ESA/NOIRLab/NSF/AURA/M.H. Wong, p. 17 (Jupiter); Naomi Rahim/Getty Images, p. 18; NASA/Bill Ingalls, p. 19; Javier Zayas Photography/Getty Images, p. 20; Christophe Lehenaff/Getty Images, p. 21; Fauzan Maududdin/EyeEm, p. 22; NASA/JPL/USGS, p. 23; DrPixel/Getty Images, p. 24; GSO Images/Getty Images, p. 25; ESO/Y. Beletsky/Wikimedia Commons, p. 26; MARK GARLICK/SCIENCE PHOTO LIBRARY/Getty Images, pp. 28, 29.

Cover: undefined undefined/Getty Images.